To Jenny +
Lots of love

June 1996

YOUNG WRITERS

ALL ABOARD FOR

BUCKINGHAMSHIRE

First published in Great Britain in 1996 by
POETRY NOW
1-2 Wainman Road, Woodston,
Peterborough, PE2 7BU

All Rights Reserved

Copyright Contributors 1996

HB ISBN 1 85731 777 7
SB ISBN 1 85731 771 8

Foreword

Toot, Toot! All Aboard! Set sail on a fantastic journey through the minds of today's children. Along the way we hope you will be charmed and enlightened by the thoughts, feelings and humour expressed by these young writers.

The poems included in this anthology have been selected for their exciting imagination, depth of feelings and down to earth language; revealing these children's awareness of various important issues close to many of our hearts. Now you can finally find out what these children *really* think of their parents, teachers and why trees lose their leaves in autumn!

We hope that you will sit back and enjoy this on-board entertainment, and we wish you a pleasant journey. Bon voyage!

CONTENTS

Great Linford County Combined School

Ruth Harley	1
Katie Ziajka	2
Christopher Thomas	2
Angharad Shaw	3
Nicola Dawson	3
Daisy Payne	4
Joshua Darke	4

Haddenham County Middle School

Sian Williams	5
Simon Smith	6
Sophie Hounslow	6
Elena Harris	7
Lee John Lloyd	8
Amanda Clarke	8
Medi Griffiths	9
Deborah Grayson	10
Vanessa Hicks	10
Margaret Johnston	11
Eddy Atkins	12
Natasha Matthews	12
Georgina Summerskill	13
Thomas Devey	14
Lucy McNeil	14
Ben Hawkins	15
Lucy Smith	16
Neil Robinson	16
Ena Matagic	17
James Veness	18
Sarah Feore	18
Aimee Hammett	19
David Rydings	20
Heather Belgrove	20
Elizabeth Griffiths	21
Colin Daly	21
Jodie Roach	22
Helen Smirthwaite	22

	Laura Pugh	23
	Sam Faul	23
	Philippa Hickman	24
	Shaun Fisher	24
	Natalie Moore	25
	Matthew Pritchard	25
	Michelle Connolly	26
	Katie Roots	26
	James Woodwards	27
	Toby Hamilton	27
	Samantha Fogden	28
	Debbie Wragg	28
	Rachel Toolan	29
	Jenny Holden	30
	Christopher Caswell	30
	Samantha Townend	31
	Stuart Wood	32
	Simon Brown	32
	Estelle Maitland	33
	Kirsty Bennett	34
	David Wainwright	35
	Tracy Rogers	36
Milton Keynes Prep School		
	Roger Davis	37
	Stuart Rowlands	37
New Bradwell County Combined School		
	Allison Searle	37
	Harriet Davis	38
	Darren Ayers	38
	Jemma Stratford	39
	Lisa Stevens	39
	Michelle Page	40
	Lyn Setchell	40
	Karma Smith	41
	Jodie Bonsell	41
	Geraint Davies	42
	Sylesh Patel	42
	Kirsty Morris	43

Oak Green CM School	Anna Maire Clare	44
	Lance Faroq	44
	Michael Robinson	45
	Simone Scarlett	45
	Liam McEnteggart	46
	Laura Haedicke	46
	Lisa Barr	47
	Craig Thornton	47
	James Mason	48
	Chris Cope	48
	Kirsty Beet	49
	Michelle Davies	49
	Aimee Read	50
	Simone Angelo	50
	Kelly Robinson	51
	Mark Edwell	52
Our Lady's RC Combined School	Hannah Potter	52
	Robert Morris	53
	Katharine Barnes	53
	Joanna Melikian	54
	Nicola Jasieniecka	54
	Latarvia Martin	55
	Sam Read	55
	Nicholas Shelley	56
	Brian Plested	56
	Chris Lander	57
	Sophie Ellis	58
	Emma Nolan	59
	Michal Hostynski	60
	Hannah Childs	60
	Thomas Hoffman	61
	Hayley Brook	61
	Joe Murphy	62
	Caroline Lapperton	62
	Matthew Parry	63
	Emily Harvey	63

	Katie Geraghty	64
	Hannah Schwerzmann	64
Robertswood County Combined School		
	Nicola Fox	65
	Joanne Gill	65
	Hayley Mitchell	66
	Thomas Duffy	66
	Greg Roberts	67
	Danny Parton	67
	Fram Dinshaw	68
	Charlotte Miles	68
	Louise Hosier	69
	Stephanie Haslam	69
	Tom Beck	70
	Tom Kirkbride	70
	Ben Doyle	71
	Virginia Follen	71
	Rebecca Galustian	72
	Sophia Collins	72
	Olivia De'ath	72
	Charlotte Richardson	73
	Samantha Earle	73
	Jonathan Slupek	74
Seer Green Combined School		
	David Lynch	74
	Laura Young	75
	Kathryn Brodie &	
	Victoria Phillips	76
	Anissa Benahmed	76
	Aleesha Adams	77
Stanton Middle School		
	Rowena Webber	77
	Vicky Lockwood	78
	Kirsten Illsley	78
	Stacy Hodgson	79
	Andrew Choy	79
	Laura Dennis	80
	Stephanie Rounce	80

	Alan Clem	81
	Tom Evison	81
	Becky Hall	81
	Craig Allen	82
	Teri Slater	82
	Dean Scott	82
	Carl Winstanley	83
	Ian Ritchie	83
	Hayley Dixon	84
	Jason Barker	84
	Brooke Fry	85
	Ashley Sharp	85
	Ben Enser	86
	Michael Fanning	86
	Lyndsey Berrie	87
	Joanne Green	87
	Laura Hammond	88
	Matthew Darton	88
	Wayne Entwistle	89
	Lewis Gardner	89
Turnfurlong Middle School		
	Ellie Wilson	90
Tylers Green Middle School		
	Nicola Cannings	90
	Naomi Telfer	91
	Joanna Thompson	91
	David Witherden	92
	Philippa Taylor	92
	Peter Thorne	93
	Hannah Jeffries	94
	Charlotte V Ellis	95
	Stephen Eakins	96

A PAINT BOX

I am going to paint you a paint box.

Take the ...
Sweet, cold grapes glistening
on the fruit dish,
the beautiful, floating scent
of the crocuses in the fresh
garden,
the light juicy plums hanging
on tropical trees,
small timid violets just peeping out from
the earth,
      That's purple!

I am going to paint you a paint box.

Take the ...
Wonderful, bright sunset on the faraway horizon,
the glistening, shiny orange on the glass
fruit dish,
the sweet smelling golden marigolds
in the fresh earth,
the juicy, ripe, shining apricots nestled
amongst the other fruit,
      That's orange!

Ruth Harley (9) Great Linford County Combined School

A PAINT BOX

I'm going to paint you a paint box,

Take the . . .
Darkness of the world. With the feeling that you
can't move, and it's creepy. You're all alone in this
world. There are evil things waiting to happen
to you.
        That's black.

Take the . . .
Peace of the world the feeling that you're
free. Everyone is cheerful including you and
me. I saw a little child that looked up
and smiled at me.
        That's white.

Katie Ziajka (9) Great Linford County Combined School

ALONE

They're dead, they're gone
I'm alone, not strong
My family they've disappeared, vanished from my life
Death is treading on my heels
Giving me trouble and strife
Nowhere to go my friends are above,
What is a life with no-one to love?

Christopher Thomas (10) Great Linford County Combined School

THE FUNERAL

The happy memories
We had are ruined by
This unhappy date
We remember thee.

Black robes, tears,
Cold, sad day.
Family and friends mourn.

Death, sadness,
Memories may make
Us cry
But we can remember
The good times, and
Forget the sad.

Angharad Shaw (10) Great Linford County Combined School

BLACK

The night comes sleek and sly
Tells the sun it's time to die.
Don't worry,
She says,
My dearest sun,
Your turn will surely come.

In the cupboard,
Under the stairs,
There's blackness all the way through
Until you turn the light on full
She'll practice tricks on you.

Nicola Dawson (10) Great Linford County Combined School

CHRISTOPHER COLUMBUS

There was a young man named Columbus,
Who sailed the sea with his compass.
Whilst on his quest,
He sailed to the west,
The adventurous Mr Columbus.

Daisy Payne (9) Great Linford County Combined School

ODYSSEUS AND POLYPHEMUS

On the island, where they grounded
And up to the cave they went.
A giant's bed, but stay instead,
And eat and drink your fill.
But as evening doth draw near
A ferocious roar do they hear.
Behind the herd comes the one-eyed death
And in the cave he comes.
He sees and eats two little men
After he has some wine,
Drugged to wash them down.
He snores and sleeps, before he wakes
A stake is in his eye.
He will see no more, for he is blind,
But he lets the sheep go by.
He feels but nothing on the top, but he can't feel underneath,
So they escape from down below,
So there's nothing he can do.
He asks his father after them,
Who is his father, who?
Poseidon is his name.

Joshua Darke (9) Great Linford County Combined School

SHE DOESN'T KNOW

She doesn't know what it feels like.
Nothing to write,
head so empty,
feeling so sad.
She just doesn't know.

She doesn't know what it feels like.
Everyone something to write,
Everyone,
Except me.
She just doesn't know.

She doesn't know what it feels like.
Tummy so empty.
Get on with your work.
How can I? With nothing to write.
She just doesn't know.

She doesn't know what it feels like.
It's not fair.
Everyone reading out work, except me.
I've got nothing, *nothing at all*.
She just doesn't know.

She doesn't know what it feels like
But . . . when you've done your work
you're proud, your head's so full.
You're going to burst.
You feel so happy,
you jump for joy.
Hip, hip, hooray.
perhaps she does know what it feels like.

Sian Williams (10) Haddenham County Middle School

ME AND MY DAD

Me and my dad are great as a team.
The fences we make look great by the stream.
The horses can't jump them,
Cows cannot eat them, but
the sheep can get through them.

Me and my dad are great as a team.
The sheds that we make are the best in the land.
The horses can sleep in them,
the sheep can eat in them,
but the cows can't.

Me and my dad are great as a team.

Simon Smith (10) Haddenham County Middle School

I THINK DAD'S AN ALIEN

I think dad's an alien
Strange things pop out of his head
He doesn't eat his food
He eats the plate instead

I think dad's an alien
He doesn't eat or drink
He plays cricket on the table
And football in the sink

I think dad's an alien
He doesn't go to bed
He chews up cardboard boxes
And wears knickers on his head

Sophie Hounslow (9) Haddenham County Middle School

BUT THAT WAS WHEN MY DAD WAS THREE

My dad was three,
Was having his tea,
Mum upstairs, watching TV.

Bored eating dinner,
Got butter, got knife,
Spread butter on . . .
Mum's new settee.

But that was when my dad was three.

Mum came down, saw the mess.
'Oh dear me,' she cried,
'Did you do it? Did you?
Are you responsible? Was it you?'

Dad sighed. 'Sorry, Mum.
Never do it again.'

Mum smacked his bottom.
He was very naughty.
The rest of the day,
His poor little bottom was . . .
Sore, sore, sore.

But that was when my dad was three.

Elena Harris (10) Haddenham County Middle School

COUCH POTATO

I went downstairs
. . . like always
Mum says
. . . like always
You're a couch potato.
Don't say that!
Oh no.
I'm a couch potato.
Mum cooked me
Then ate me whole!
It was very dark in mum.
I lit a match.
Then . . .
She spat me out.
I flew across the room . . .
Like a bullet.
Smash
Bang
Splattered
Sliding down the wall.

Lee John Lloyd (10) Haddenham County Middle School

I HATE MATHS TESTS

'Miss, Miss,
I don't have 17 fingers.'
'Use your toes then,'
'Yes Miss.'

'Miss, Miss
I don't have 28 fingers and toes.'
'Hurry up Amanda.'
'Yes Miss.'

'That's all,' she says, 'Hurry up Amanda.'
'All maths tests in.'
'Oh no! I haven't even done two!'

Amanda Clarke (9) Haddenham County Middle School

NEARLY EXTINCT

The panda bear eats bamboo,
   he's nearly extinct.
The tiger hunts in the jungle,
   he's nearly extinct.
The elephant herd strides across sandy land,
   they're nearly extinct.
The beautiful parrot sits in a tree,
   he's nearly extinct too.
All these animals have a right to live.
   Just like we do.

People kill the panda bear for fur,
People kill the tiger for fur and bones,
People kill the parrot for feathers,
People kill the elephants for tusks.

I wish people would leave them all alone,
So they can live in peace.
Because I know . . .
If they become extinct,
We might soon be extinct too.

Medi Griffiths (10) Haddenham County Middle School

NEW YORK

All alone,
In your world,
No-one knows you,
No-one cares,
There are eight million people,
How can you feel lonely?
They're all as lost,
With nowhere to turn,
No-one to give a helping hand.
There are eight million people,
How can you feel lonely?
Your problems are yours,
And you realise, bitterly,
That no-one,
Is going,
To come.
Eight million people,
All the same,
Bitterly lonely,
'Cause nobody came.
Eight million people,
Now all feeling lonely.

Deborah Grayson (10) Haddenham County Middle School

MY HAMSTER

Scratch, scratch,
Nibble, nibble,
That's the sound my hamster makes.

Little and furry.
Nice and soft.
Soft and squidgy.

Cuddle, cuddle.
Stroke, stroke.
I love my hamster.

Vanessa Hicks (9) Haddenham County Middle School

GUESS WHAT?

Guess what?
What?
I learnt to drive when I was two!

No never.
Yeah.
It's true. Let me tell you.

We came home from Tesco's
Mum got out of the car.
Right now's my chance.

Out of my car seat I scrambled
Seat belt on, door shut,
All ready.

Now.
Mum's opened the garage door.
Right. Now it's my turn.

Key's turned, pedal down.
Wow! What an experience.

Through one side out the other.
You should try it, you should.

Guess what?
What?
Nothing.

Margaret Johnston (10) Haddenham County Middle School

SPLASH

My brother swings over the river.
Ben swings over the river.
I try to swing over the river.
I'm swinging, I'm swinging
Dad catch me!
I'm
   s
    l
     ip
      pin
     g
         I'm
           sl
             ip
               pin
                 g

Splash

I'm walking home.
Walking like a wet
Gorilla
Says Ben.

What's mum going to say.

Eddy Atkins (10) Haddenham County Middle School

THE DOUBLE DECKER BUS

It's the biggest bus
I've ever seen,
It stops just by
the village green.

I mean it is,
it's really tall,
Can't say much about
the one for school.

I've never ever been on it,
although I know I should.
Mum's been on it loads of times
she says it's very good.

Natasha Matthews (9) Haddenham County Middle School

THE SCHOOL TV

Everybody's waiting to watch TV.
Language programme
    Yippee!

Teacher turns on the TV
    Nothing!

Tries again
    Nothing!

Someone's broken the TV
Why?
Oh, why?

Someone's broken the TV
What a thing to do.

I bet you think so too?

Don't you?

Georgina Summerskill (9) Haddenham County Middle School

WAITING IN THE HOSPITAL

Waiting in the hospital.
Wait, wait, wait.
Come on Doctor, I don't want to be
Late, late, late.

Waiting in the hospital.
I hope it won't be long.
I know,
I'll just sing a little song.

Waiting in the hospital.
Ah, it's time,
William,
Stop doing that mime.

Waiting in the hospital.
Need an x-ray
Please don't tell me it's broken
I pray, I pray, I pray.

Waiting in the hospital.
Going home to tell dad
Ow, ow, ow.
It hurts very
Bad!

Thomas Devey (10) Haddenham County Middle School

MY DAD

    My dad's name is Billy,
    and he's a bit silly,
    so I call him silly Billy,

My dad likes watching Mr Bean,
so I call him silly Bean,

> My dad's friend is called
> silly Ben so I call them,
> Bill and Ben the silly men,

My dad likes watching *Bottom*,
so I call him silly *Bottom*,

> So altogether he's a silly
> Billy Bottom Bean Ben!

Lucy McNeil (10) Haddenham County Middle School

THE MINI

Let's go in the Mini,
Go on,
Hop in,
I'll drive.

Starting up,
Clatter, clatter,
Bang, bang.

Taking off,
What's that noise?
Wheel falling off!
Don't worry
There it goes now.

What's that noise?
Don't worry.
Door falling off.
There it goes now.

What's that noise?
Worry,
Mini's blowing up
There it goes.

Ben Hawkins (10) Haddenham County Middle School

TEACHERS

Teachers are so bossy,
moaning all the time,
nagging everyone.

Nag, nag, nag, nag, nag.
I told you to do that yesterday,
why haven't you done it.
Go and do it now.

You're meant to sharpen them at home.
Why didn't you do it,
quickly do it now.

Time for spellings!
Shhhh
Be quiet Natasha Matthews.
Wrong, wrong, wrong, wrong, wrong,
all wrong.
Why didn't you learn
your *spellings?*
Ten out of ten, out of ten,
Nothing but ten out of ten will do.

Lucy Smith (9) Haddenham County Middle School

MY DAD

My dad is a funny dad.
Yesterday he stuck his arm to the
desk and got a bit stressed.
He really tried his best but he
could not get away.
We had to call the fire brigade to
take apart the desk.

Today he had a driving test.
He tried his best and crashed on
his test.
We had to call the fire brigade
(again)
They got him out, now my dad stays in.

Neil Robinson (10) Haddenham County Middle School

MY LITTLE PUPPY

Got a silly little puppy.
He chases sheep and barks.

Got a silly little puppy.
Likes being stroked, played with
and walked.

Got a silly little puppy
He's sometimes jealous of me.

Don't know why.
Maybe . . . because mum
cuddles me.

Got a silly little puppy
He jumps, he barks
to get my mum's attention.

When mum sees him
she has to stroke him.

Got a silly little puppy.
I love him very much.

Ena Matagic (10) Haddenham County Middle School

MY DAD

My dad's a nice guy,
He always plays with me,
Hardly ever mad, always happy, never sad.

Playing cricket,
Ball over fence,
Normal dad mad,
But not my dad, he isn't mad.

Playing snooker,
Cue broken,
Normal dad mad,
But not my dad, he isn't mad.

Running in the living room,
Oops, a vase,
Normal dad mad,
But not my dad, he isn't mad.

Playing tennis, ball hits dad
Normal dad mad,
But he isn't mad.

But that's dad for you.

James Veness (10) Haddenham County Middle School

I THINK MY MUM'S A HIPPY

I think my mum's a hippy,
She has curly wurly hair,
She dyed it pink and orange, with
a golden lock of hair

I think my mum's a hippy,
She had a motorbike, coloured
purple, blue and white

I think my mum's a hippy,
but I really don't care, for that's her
way, a hippy way, she's really not
to blame

I think my mum's a hippy,
but she's an only mum, so you really
can't blame her, for
what she has done.

Sarah Feore (10) Haddenham County Middle School

MAYHEM IN THE CLASSROOM

One day Miss went to do some photocopying
And . . .
Mayhem in the classroom,
I didn't know what to do,
Bobby Bone was singing,
Jessie needs the loo,
A wet patch on the carpet,
Just to match the wall,
And take my word for it mate,
That's not all,
Mickey Moore's doing his times tables on the floor,
When Miss finds out she's going to start a war,
So maybe it wasn't that important to do
The photocopying after all.

Aimee Hammett (10) Haddenham County Middle School

ANIMALS

I like animals because they're
>   soft and scary
>   scary and hairy
>   hairy and furry
>   chubby and grubby
>   small and tall
>   brill and they can kill
>   they can fly and cry
>   fight and bite

Most of all I like animals

David Rydings (9) Haddenham County Middle School

THE PLANET MARS

The planet Mars is a dark and
gloomy place,
My head is like the planet Mars.
All closed up, nowhere to go,
Pretend friends, pretend friends,
Forever in my mind,
Pretend friends, pretend friends,
Repeating over and over,
No-one to like me,
No-one to care,
The world should be changed,
No war,
Just friendship everywhere.

Heather Belgrove (10) Haddenham County Middle School

SHOE LACES

Don't you find it funny,
that when you do up your shoe laces,
your hands help each other.
I imagine that my hands can talk.
One's called Rosie and the other one's Fred.
One morning they were helping each other.
'I put that over there'
said Rosie.
'Do I go over there?'
said Fred
'I make a loop and you go round'
'Now we pull'
said Fred.
Shall we tie the other one? . . .

Elizabeth Griffiths (10) Haddenham County Middle School

WINTER

Winter is a special time of year
The snow falls gently on the ground
The children play outside
Building snowmen
Snow for the body
Snow for the head
Stones for the mouth and eyes
A carrot for the nose
People sledging down a hill
Snowballs flying
Roads are slippy round the town
Fires burning in every little house and cottage
Winter is a special time of year

Colin Daly (10) Haddenham County Middle School

I'VE GOT A COLD!

My nose needs blowing,
I've got a cold!

My eyes are watering,
I've got a cold!

I've got a headache,
I've got a cold!

Oh no my tummy hurts,
I've got a cold!

I can't talk my throat hurts,
I've got a cold!

I can't hear,
I've got a cold!

My mum asks what's the matter?
She's got a cold!

Jodie Roach (10) Haddenham County Middle School

MY POEM

I'm trying to think of a poem
But I'm finding it very difficult.
You see I've never thought of myself being a poet.
I've tried things like:-
One day it was nice and sunny but it rained.
No, that sounds silly, or
My favourite colour's purple but I think about orange.
No, that sounds silly too. I know one.
I'm trying to think of a poem
But I'm finding it very difficult,
You see

Helen Smirthwaite (10) Haddenham County Middle School

SALLY'S BEEN LOOKING FAT

Sally's been looking fat
Why?
I don't understand it
Sally's looking fatter every day.
Why?
I woke up one morning ready for school.
So!
I came back and Sally wasn't in her basket
Yeh!
I looked everywhere when it came to tea time
I looked in the cupboard
Yeh!
Sally was there
Oh!
But wait.
Why?
She had puppies
Aah!

Laura Pugh (10) Haddenham County Middle School

MY POEM

When I was about five,
my gran and grandad were at my house.
Holly was chasing me,
through the hall,
round the table,
back through the hall,
out through the dining room
and *smash* I jumped through a
glass door and landed on my bum laughing,
and everyone said Sam are you alright.

Sam Faul (9) Haddenham County Middle School

DEAR STEP MUM

That dress you sent me in the post is lovely.
(The flowers on it are awful)

And the socks to match are a lovely colour.
(Little frilly pink socks yuk!)

And some adorable pink satin slippers and hair band
(The dress is enormous and it's for little kids and I'm 15)

I showed it to my friends at school
(They hated it)

Mum said I shouldn't wear it at dinner
(But I do, oh no! I spilt my dinner down it what a shame)

Your
(Not)
Ever loving
Philippa

Philippa Hickman (10) Haddenham County Middle School

THE FARMER

Every day at 7 o'clock the tractors
Brum
Brum
Every day at 7 o'clock my dad's working
Moving the bails, feeding the cows and cleaning
out the muck
    Smelly
    Smelly
    Moo, moo
go the cows every day, I'm awake
listening to the radio.

Shaun Fisher (10) Haddenham County Middle School

IT'S RAINING CATS AND DOGS

I went outside to play
just as it started to rain.
A most peculiar sight was
in front of my eyes -
it was raining cats and dogs.
White cats, black cats,
tabby, grey and ginger cats
falling from the sky
labradors, collies and retrievers
falling from the sky
cats and dogs falling in puddles
it's really raining cats and dogs.

Natalie Moore (10) Haddenham County Middle School

MY DAD DOESN'T WANT TO GO TO SCHOOL

My dad doesn't want to go to school today
Plan A, he pretends to be ill
But oh no that doesn't work.

Plan B run into the toilet and lock the door

Yes his mum can't get in, yes.
Oh no I can't get out

'Mum, mum I can't get out'

'Hang on love I'll get the neighbour round'

Stand back
Smash
'Mum I don't want to go to school today'
'You're not
It's bank holiday'
All because my dad doesn't want to go to school

Matthew Pritchard (10) Haddenham County Middle School

SPACE

When I look up at the stars,
I think to myself,
What is up there, black and more black
Or a land of make-believe
With lollipops as pens
And pens and paper round wrong way
I would love to see
My land of dreams

What would my mum say to my land of make-believe?
Oh, it's a lot of nonsense, or so I believe.

Michelle Connolly (10) Haddenham County Middle School

SCHOOL

The best part of the day is always grey.
So why do I have to stay all day?
Why, why is school so boring?
I don't know, because I'm snoring.
Screams are everywhere like a beam.
You should come and see what I mean.
Work, work is all we do
The teachers don't know what we are going through.
Running about is what we do
At playtime we have a great time
I wish school was cool.
Hey Miss how about a pool in the school?
Only when I win the jackpot.
Now do you see why school is so boring
That's why I'm always snoring.

Katie Roots (10) Haddenham County Middle School

TEACHERS

Teachers, they are so mean, all they give us
is a bean.

But when they go out the room, we party
like wild baboons.

They make us come in after 10 minutes
of games.

Then all we do is listen to the trains.

We sit in our classroom working hard.

Writing on paper and mounting card.

I do my homework sometimes at
school .

So all weekend I can play football.

James Woodwards (10) Haddenham County Middle School

MY CAT

One day my cat saw a rat
it chased it and chased it until my
cat ate it. My cat was very hasty,
but I bet he thought it was tasty.
He came in after supper and me and him
played with my puppet.
After my supper me and my cat went for a walk
We saw two boys having a talk.
We also saw two sheep and then a car went *beep beep*
It was my mum she came because it was my bedtime.
When we got home me and my cat did a mime.

Toby Hamilton (10) Haddenham County Middle School

I HATE SCHOOL

I hate school
it is boring.
Miss I need the toilet.
Miss my pencil disappeared.
Once I fell asleep in lessons.
Miss I've got no paper
Miss I feel ill so can I go home?
One morning I sat at the table
thinking whoever came up with
the idea of school must be crazy.

It was near lunchtime and that
is the worst part of the day.
Apples go flying round the room.

Samantha Fogden (10) Haddenham County Middle School

THE PHANTOM HORSE

The phantom horse roaming free,
Galloping over the land and sea,
Through the silver moonlit night,
His pale coat shining ghostly white.

The phantom horse strong and fast,
Racing as he gallops past,
He always seems to win the race,
Even the wind can't match his pace.

The phantom horse rearing high,
Stretching hard to reach the sky,
His grey mane flying long and wide,
And his tail flowing by his side.

Debbie Wragg (10) Haddenham County Middle School

ME AND MY FRIEND

Me and my friend Jim,
We love going to the park,
We act just like kids,
Playing on the swings and the roundabout,
Sometimes,
If we're lucky,
We get an ice-cream,
Always the same flavour,
Vanilla, with a chocolate flake,
After that we go on the seesaw
One day me and Jim were on the slide,
It's a really tall one that goes round
in a spiral,
Me and Jim usually meet each other
at the bottom,
But that day Jim went first,
I was standing at the top waiting
for him to call my name
Instead of hearing a Jonny
I heard a waaa . . .
I climbed down the steps and saw
Jim at the bottom clutching his leg,
I ran all the way home to tell my mum
She came in the car,
She said his leg was broken,
We took him to hospital,
Now he's got his leg in plaster,
I went to the park this morning,
Going down the slide didn't seem
the same.

Rachel Toolan (10) Haddenham County Middle School

PLAN 49

Alfie my cat wanted his dinner so he tried Plan 49.
All he had to do is climb a tree and sit down to dine.
He licked his lips and climbed the
tree, and thinks of a juicy bird.
Maybe a plump sparrow or juicy starling,
but then the worst sound ever heard
He sees a blackbird fly away.
The fattest one ever seen.
Worse still, as the bird flies, he warns
the others with a scream.
He spots a bird at the end of a twig
and sneaks behind secretly.
Just a few more steps along the branch
and then he could have his tea.
The branch starts to bend beneath his weight.
He tries to step back but it's just too late.
The branch cracks and breaks and down he goes
'Youch' he cries as he lands on his nose
Alfie my cat never got to dine
And out of his lives he's lost eight out of nine.

Jenny Holden (10) Haddenham County Middle School

LATE FOR SCHOOL

First it started
My brother and me,
We're late again,
Oh goodness me

A slam of the gate,
A shout we're late
Oh goodness me
Oh goodness me

We're in the car
Not going very far
Oh goodness me
Oh goodness me

We got a lift
Went quite fast
We got to school
It's only quarter past eight.

Christopher Caswell (10) Haddenham County Middle School

GOING HOME

It's the end of school now,
It's a quarter past two,
I'm really happy,
because I'm dying for the loo.
Ddrriinngg! Goes the bell,
So we all rush out of class.
Ooh hang on a minute Aimee,
I've dropped my bus pass.
I find one under my chair,
but it's not mine.
Mine's over there,
I'm packing up my bag now,
I swing it over my shoulder.
Ha ha! The boy in front of me,
he looks like a little tin soldier.
I'm going out the door now.
I'm free! I'm free! I'm free!
I'm running out of school now,
I can't wait until my tea.

Samantha Townend (10) Haddenham County Middle School

DINO - BABY'S FIRST DAY OUT

This afternoon I was going to a cartoon,
The cartoon was bad but really quite sad,
I went out crying and started sighing.
I went to the pub and wanted to stay
But they kicked me out and I began to shout.
I said to myself I can't wait till I'm old and
Very bold.
I went home to dad to get in my bed
But my dad was playing with my Ted.
I said to my dad I had a wonderful day
But the only thing is - I couldn't pay.
      Wa Wa Wa!

Stuart Wood (10) Haddenham County Middle School

MY DOGS

I have two dogs
One is lazy
One is crazy
One is pasty
One is hasty

I have two dogs
One is a puppy
One has puppies
One has a bed
One sleeps in the shed
One swims
One wins

Simon Brown (10) Haddenham County Middle School

MITTENS

My pet Mittens,
Is one of many kittens,
But none are quite the same.

He eats voles,
And digs holes,
Runs from balls and,
Leaves leaves in halls.

He is now quite fat,
For an average type cat,
He never seems to run,
And will eat anything from a fish to a bun.

At six in the morning,
He'll stop my dad snoring,
And squeaks for his breakfast,
Along with his brother,
Who seems like his mother!

Although he doesn't seem like the greatest,
Or the very latest
But to me he's the best kitty.

Estelle Maitland (10) Haddenham County Middle School

ANIMALS

Bitsy the hamster is chubby. She is multi-coloured
and her brother is Teeny Weeny.

Teeny Weeny is brown with a black patch on
his head. All he does is lie in bed..

Teeny Weeny loves escaping. All he does is
Drive me mad while Itsy sits there. She
is lazy.

Fish, fish, fish, we have some fish
as well as hamsters.

They swim all day, they fight at night.
One lays eggs the rest eat them.

My fish are rich silver and gold. Even for
£100, they wouldn't be sold.
My fish are bold in the cold, some are
young, some are old.

I love my fish, I love my hamsters.
But when they are ill we go to the vets.
I feed my fish, I play with my hamsters
Usually at sunset.

Kirsty Bennett (9) Haddenham County Middle School

UFO ON HOLIDAY

A UFO passed one day
All the people ran away
because they thought he would
Stay
But he was on holiday.

The UFO was blue and
Striped
And he carried dynamite
The UFO came up to me
So I ran up a tree.

So we had a conversation
Then I ran to the Station
Then I hopped onto a train
But he thought it was a game

So I legged it down the road
But he forgot his
Green cross code

This poem happened in Dover
And he was knocked down
By a Rover

David Wainwright (10) Haddenham County Middle School

TV PRESENTERS

TV presenters are chatty people
All they care about are. . .
Silly shows
Chatter on
Boring all watchers

        Sigh! Sigh!
        Yawn, yawn
        What a day
        Boring calls
        Every day the same
        Chatter, chatter
        Blah! Blah!

I'm so silly to come
I'll never come again . . .
Never again to listen to . . .

Blah! Blah!
Chatter, chatter,
    All I do is
        Yawn!

I sit there eating carrots
I must be mad
I don't even like them!

Tracy Rogers (10) Haddenham County Middle School

MY ROOM

I wish my room had a floor
A window, a desk and a door
When using the loo,
I always fall through,
And I can't stand it anymore.

Roger Davis (10) Milton Keynes Prep School

THE SUMMER SUN

The summer sun
Can be very fun
Children play, jump and run
Chasing butterflies,
Picking flowers
They'll stay in fields for hours and hours

Stuart Rowlands (10) Milton Keynes Prep School

HELP BADGERS

Badger,
Slow, staring, sleepy,
Muddy, dirty
Why do we kill them just for their fur?
Badger

Allison Searle (10) New Bradwell County Combined School

HEDGEHOGS

As night draws on the sun gone in,
A hedgehog's crawling past the bin.
He scuffles loudly on the lawn,
When finally the broken dawn,
Awakes the birds, begin to sing,
It's 4am the church bells ring,
Chinks of light bring on the day
The dazzled hedgehog shrinks away
He hurries back into the trees,
Before the night is all deceased.
Inside the house some noise is heard,
And in the trees a noisy bird,
He hides beneath some leaves and twigs,
And forages and then he digs.
And then he meets his hedgehog mate,
They scuffle quietly through the gate.
The hedgehogs basking in the sun,
Another day has just begun.

Harriet Davis (11) New Bradwell County Combined School

THE BATH

I am a boy who loves having baths.
When I sink into the water it feels
like I'm walking on a long path,
Just thinking of all the things
that worry me.
I lose all my fears finally.
I was once scared of water
and scared I would drown
but I know I won't go down.

Darren Ayers (11) New Bradwell County Combined School

HEDGEHOGS

Hedgehogs
>They all have long snouts
>to sniff things out
>but when people are around
>they sleep safe and sound.

We see hedgehogs
>at night when it's not light
>and in the morning
>they're all snoring

When it's time
>for the hedgehogs to eat
>they go to houses for cat meat.

Jemma Stratford (11) New Bradwell County Combined School

WHEN A FRIEND GOES

Bye, bye said she,
I'm sorry it's me,
But I'm off to see the world.
What wonders I face,
as I dash and I race to see
- this wonderful world
Don't worry said she
I'll write back to thee
Oh, goodbye for now!

Lisa Stevens (11) New Bradwell County Combined School

THE TREE

The tree grows high in the sky
The birds sit on the branches
Going *cheep cheep cheep!*
The branches swaying this way and
That when the wind blows.
The leaves are as green as grass
The trunk is as brown as the mud
Oh, look at that beautiful tree.

Michelle Page (11) New Bradwell County Combined School

SCARY NIGHTS

Underneath the table where I don't like to sleep
Spiders creep,
Windows creak,
Caged in.
When bombs go off I try to hide.

Hitler's secret weapons are flying overhead.
Super fast
Engine drops,
Silence.
Who will Hitler's victims be tonight?

The greatest mega weapon is about to strike.
Golf ball size.
Hatch opens,
Descent.
Damage as great as five thousand raids.

Lyn Setchell (10) New Bradwell County Combined School

THE ARMADILLO

The Armadillo that you see
Is protected from head to knee

They feed on small insects
And a lot of other stuff.

When the Armadillos fight they
Are very rough
With their long claws and quite sharp
Teeth

But I say they are lovely
No matter what people think.

Karma Smith (10) New Bradwell County Combined School

WAR POEM

The Anderson is shaking,
The bombs are going off,
Everyone is very scared.
People screaming,
Planes are flying overhead.

Outside it's very dark,
Streets are destroyed,
Soldiers in the streets with guns,
Bodies are scattered everywhere,
A very scary sight.

War is nearly over,
Hitler is nearly gone,
Soon everyone will be happy,
We can now get on with our lives,
Victory's nearly done.

Jodie Bonsell (11) New Bradwell County Combined School

WORLD WAR

I draw myself to the action
German planes roaring over head
People stop and listen
As I hear the bomb falling
All people can do is hope

People try to get to safety
but it is too late to run and hide
the bomb has exploded
Screams of pain surround me
As the *'boom'* comes back to me
I wonder 'Why did it start.'

Millions have died in the war
Loved ones buried under houses
thousands of people homeless
and all because of Hitler
Who never thought about the consequences
of *World War!*

Geraint Davies (10) New Bradwell County Combined School

WORLD WAR II

Children evacuated
To somewhere free from bombs
They're on the train
Leaving London what a shame
With their own brown gas mask on
One toy, one shirt and socks.

Children sitting on the train
Hoping for dads to be there
Staring at open field
Away from the big city
To a quiet country living
Children got off the train

Children are all safely there
Farm, food, cows, ducks and play
Children love this new way
From time to time they shed tear
Thinking of their lost parents
Dreaming of safe homes.

Sylesh Patel (11) New Bradwell County Combined School

A CHILD DURING THE WAR

Underground in a shelter,
Bombs coming down like rain,
Wondering what's happening it disturbs most people
I bet we will have to rebuild the city,
My dad is probably dead,
I just wish this war was not happening and I was in my bed.

My dad is in the Army,
I think having a war is crazy.
I hope the war is going to end soon.
Aeroplanes zooming and crashing,
The houses are crashing too.
I hope our house is still up.

1945 the war has ended *hurray!*
The city has been wrecked,
Just the same as our lives,
Hitler's gone, we have won,
I hope the war does not happen again.

Kirsty Morris (11) New Bradwell County Combined School

SQUIRRELS

Squirrels,
Busy, fat, thin,
Red, grey,
The red squirrels run away.
Squirrels.

Anna Maire Clare (11) New Bradwell County Combined School

SPRING TIME

The soft flaky tree
Rose high above the dull loam,
It's captivating perfume coming from
The pure white velvety petals
Overflowing in a fountain of leaves
and flowers.
The blooming tree
Standing, still like a wonderful
statue.
Petals fragile and flimsy,
Bark, it's texture rough and peeling.
The colour dark and dull.
Contrasting with showers of
snowflakes
Dropping faintly from the tallest
branches
Which were reaching from the tallest
branches
Which were reaching up for heaven.
The petals now falling,
The blossom is dying.
The petals lie on the dull loam
Rotting until next year.

Lance Faroq (10) Oak Green CM School

AUTUMN

All leaves fall off trees,
Use them for a compost heap
Then play in them.
Use them for a camp.
My mum helps me put them
on a bonfire.
Next autumn do the same
thing again.
Same thing probably happens
in Thame

Michael Robinson (11) Oak Green CM School

WALKING ALONE AT NIGHT

I'm walking alone in the dark
With only the trees for company
They stand towering over me
Their ghostly figures frozen by the cold autumn wind.

There are tiny glass pearls on the grass below
Reflecting the light of the moon
That sits in the sky watching me
With his army of glittering stars.

There are spooky sounds around me
They fill my mind with dread
I scream, but no-one hears me
Only the moon is there
But he's too far away to hear the cries
Of a small boy, alone in the dark.

Simone Scarlett (11) Oak Green CM School

SPRING TIME

Blossoms are fountains of
Fragrance, flowing down
Streams of beautiful colours,
Soon the blossoms fall off the
trees,
Like a waterfall
Splashing onto the floor.

Liam McEnteggart (10) Oak Green CM School

SPRING

In spring, branches brown and crisp
Have blossom bursting out like
fountains
Each tree covers another
Like a great blanket of patchwork.
White blossom falls to the ground
like a carpet of snow
Pink and cherry red blossom fall
abundantly
As confetti at a wedding
Covering new spring grass underneath
Speckled with daisy, dandelion and
bluebell
Their heads thrusting through the
soil softly.
The sweet smell like roses.
Small animals come out of hibernation
to see the wonder of spring.

Laura Haedicke (9) Oak Green CM School

SPRING

High trees waving in the sky,
Blossoms falling down.
Like snowflakes.
Lovely colours,
Pink, red, cream and white.
Dark cherry red.
The sunshine makes the blossom stand out.
Tree trunks high in the sky with
blossoms on top.
Trees waving, children jumping up.
Knocking the blossoms off,
Beautiful blossoms.
Everyone likes blossoms.

Lisa Barr (10) Oak Green CM School

SPRING

It's spring at last.
Trees covered in pink and white blossom.
Blended together in splendour.
Like fountains cascading
Falling like pink puffy marshmallow.
White blossom falling gently
Like soft snowflakes.
Trees which look like fountains
Of water which is lovely and dazzling.
Overflowing with beautiful
Clouds of blossom.

Craig Thornton (9) Oak Green CM School

THE SNAKE

A snake came to my wishing well
last night.
It slowly slithered through the
long grass.
It swiftly slid up the old brick
wall.
And sipped up some water from the
old tin bucket.
The long muscular snake twisted
away into the warm mid-summer's
night.

James Mason (9) Oak Green CM School

A SNAKE POEM

Something came to our classroom
today,
A narrow, thin, slimy snake came,
A pleasant snake that slipped
through my hands,
Kindly, shocking snake slithered
out of the bag,
Excited children slowly opened
their mouths with apprehension.

Chris Cope (9) Oak Green CM School

THE SNAKE

A snake came to our classroom.
It was fascinating to see it's red
and black tongue flickering out like
a fork.
The body has dark colours and a slim
body.
His head is hard and scaly like
a dinosaurs nose,
His eyes are like red larva.
His body has got a symmetrical
pattern with the odd spot.
The texture of the snake is bumpy
and rough.
He is very thin so he can't eat
small mice or a baby bird.
The texture of his skin is like a
magical rainforest.

Kirsty Beet (9) Oak Green CM School

SPRINGTIME

In spring, beautiful blossom is
opening like pink butterflies
flapping in the sun.
Or purple sweets raining from
the sky.
The pink and white blossom.
Like fountains of white cream
soda . . .

Michelle Davies (10) Oak Green CM School

SPRING

The pink cherry and white
bouquet of blossom.
The soft silky touch hold a
fragrance of freshness and the
glory of a spring day.
The beauty of the fragile petals
flow like a mass of
multi-coloured snow.
A beautiful blend of blossom
bending the branches.
Every flower looks prettier as
the bright sun shines it light.

Aimee Read (10) Oak Green CM School

MISS, MISS

Miss, miss
I've lost my rubber
and I can't find another.

Miss, miss
I can't find this
I've lost the times table list

Miss, miss
What's the time?
I can't get my poem to rhyme

Miss, miss
is it time to go home?
I don't want to walk on my
Own!

Simone Angelo (11) Oak Green CM School

BLOSSOM

Springtime blossom is here every year,
But only in the spring.
Clouds of pure, fresh petals,
To us they bring.

Blossom is a delightful,
Glorious mountain of cherry
and snow,
With its smooth white petals,
And fragrance as the wind
blows.

Not forgetting the cherry
blossom,
That has a delicate scent.
It is very joyful when it opens,
A sign of spring is what it
meant.

But soon it comes to,
Blossom fading away.
And gently like a snowfall,
Drops until another day.

Kelly Robinson (10) Oak Green CM School

SID THE SNAKE

One day, Korin's dad came to the classroom.
'What's coming?' I say, 'A snake!'
I was so eager to touch it, I
couldn't wait.
At last I got to hold her scaly,
muscular body.
She weaved silently out of my hands
towards my friend.
In out, in out, her sensitive tongue
searched for food.
Her rubbery drift swayed and glides.
Her willowy tail waved through the air.
Her swift narrow head is like a jet.
The thin bumpy skin wriggles in terror.
As she gets hot and bothered.
Her staring eyes, as black as night,
Never blinked as she searched for her prey.

Mark Edwell (10) Oak Green CM School

MY PET RABBIT

I've always wanted a little pet rabbit
That's beautifully pink all over,
It's soft, squeezy, cuddly and warm
It makes a quiet rustling noise as it
walks around in his cage,
It eats all of the cabbage and drinks
all of the water.
I really would love a little pet rabbit.

Hannah Potter (10) Our Lady's RC Combined School

I'M GOING TO BE A FOOTBALLER

I'm going to be a footballer one day
The best of the best with trophies locked up,
away.
I'm definitely going to be a footballer one day
Brilliant players around me when I play
Roaring crowds, swaying flags, banners with my name
I'm going to be a footballer one day
I really hope it goes that way.

Robert Morris (10) Our Lady's RC Combined School

THE RACE

I get really nervous before a running race,
I start shivering then my eyes water.
We line up for the race.
Then the gun goes *bang*
And we're off.
The wind's rushing through my hair,
My heart's pounding,
I'm really hot.
The trees are racing by,
My legs are tired out and turning into jelly.
I can see the tape in the distance.
Someone's running up behind me and overtakes,
I run faster and get back in front of her.
The race has nearly finished.
I come through the tape first
I've done it!

Katharine Barnes (10) Our Lady's RC Combined School

THE PLAY

Before performing on stage in a theatre,
My tummy is turning over and over,
5,4,3,2,1 and it's time to go on to the stage,
I start singing with three other people and selling flags
for the audience to wave, and then everything is easy,
All my characters go well,
But I'm sad it's over.

Joanna Melikian (10) Our Lady's RC Combined School

I'M WAITING

I wish Emily would go on holiday
I wish she'd go away
It's not that I don't like her
But then *they'd* come and stay.

I'd play with them every day
I bet I wouldn't lose them
My mum would go crackers
If they went astray.

They're very small
Mum calls them rodents
I think they're really cute

Two mice and a hamster
They're Emily's pets
I really cannot wait

Nicola Jasieniecka (10) Our Lady's RC Combined School

BROTHERS AND SISTERS

My brother is a pain.
He always calls me names.
He's punching, shouting, kicking too.
My dog's barking,
My mum is shouting,
My sister's fighting and dad is at work.

'I'm back from work!' shouts dad.
He comes in the room and he hears,
the noise.
He shouts *Stop it.*
The noise goes down then it starts again.

Latarvia Martin (9) Our Lady's RC Combined School

TESTS

When I have a test
I get all worked up,
And then start sweating,
And biting my nails.

When I have a test,
I get really nervous,
And then start shivering,
And knocking my knees.

When I have a test,
I worry so much,
And then start staring
But come on it's only a *test!*

When I've done a test,
I feel dead relieved,
I just feel that I've come out of hell
And I know, that I tried well!

Sam Read (10) Our Lady's RC Combined School

THE FIGHTS

Whatever I say when a fight comes
along whatever I do, whatever I suggest
I'm always in the wrong,
They moan and moan and to
me that's all they say,
I may as well give into them, they
always get their way.
I just sit back and watch them
take everything, like a piece of
cake and the empty room is left
for me to do what I want with
All I see, It's not fair!

Nicholas Shelley (10) Our Lady's RC Combined School

SISTERS

Has this ever happened to you?
You get blamed for something
you haven't done.
Like when Kate forgot to
record a programme, she
blamed me for that.
And mum always
believes her.
That's the thing with
older sisters - they always
get their way.
But when you're a younger
brother you can get away
with quite a lot of things too.
Like asking mum for
some money to buy sweets
but Kate should have
her own money.

Brian Plested (9) Our Lady's RC Combined School

WALKING THE DOG

When I walk my dog
In the mornings of the weekends
I feel scared
When I walk down the alley.

There's a broken fence
With a sheet of plastic over it
And when the wind blows
It makes a ghostly noise which makes me hurry.

I skid round the corner
To a big clump of trees
I look about me
And I see eyes looking at every move I make.

I finally come out
Onto the field.
I let my dog off the lead.
I'm not scared out there.

I turn around to look back
I think about the way home.
I have to go back in there.
I'm glad I've got my dog with me.

Chris Lander (10) Our Lady's RC Combined School

THE WEDDING

It is the night before the wedding,
I can't wait until the day,
The Bride and Groom came over,
I'm a bridesmaid on the day,
That's why I'm so afraid.

It's the day of the wedding,
We're driving to the church,
I'm in a lovely bridesmaid's dress,
We're at the church already,
I'm getting so afraid.

I'm walking up the aisle behind the bride,
We're at the bottom of the church,
The wedding goes on and on
We're going to the reception
To have a lovely meal

It's the end of the reception,
We had a lovely time,
We're going to the evening do
To have seomething to eat.
I'm getting so excited.

We're at the evening do,
We're having something to eat
I'm dancing with my sister and cousin
The wedding was really fun
I'd like to go to another.

Sophie Ellis (9) Our Lady's RC Combined School

THE EXCITEMENT

It's the evening before my birthday
I'm going to be ten
I'm going to have some friends around
We're going to build a den.

We're going to have a barbecue
It's going to be really neat
We're going to eat and eat and eat
And then we'll eat some more

It's night time but I can't stop thinking of what's
in store for me
Tomorrow when they come around
I'll have to wait and see

It's time for bed
I'm really excited
I feel like jumping on my bed to get rid of some energy
I turn on the light to do some reading
And fall asleep without realising.

It's the next morning
I can't stop myself
I run into my mum's room and shout
'It's my birthday.'

I have loads of stuff
From large to small
The end of my birthday.
I enjoyed every minute
Now I can't wait till next year

Emma Nolan (10) Our Lady's RC Combined School

IT'S NOT THERE

It is a Saturday morning and I am eating my breakfast
My mum comes up to me and tells me we are going to
the toy shop
'Can't I get a Pog Mega Pack?'
'Well I suppose so!'
So we get into the car and drive to the toy shop
We go in and see no Pog Mega Packs
I am really sad and mad.
We look all over the shop and still don't find any
I am so annoyed
I go home really annoyed and sad.

Michal Hostynski (10) Our Lady's RC Combined School

THE CROSS COUNTRY RACE

It's the start of a race at cross country
I'm really nervous
I'm doing my warm ups
I've got 10 minutes
We are all lining up now at the start
I'm really really nervous now
Bang!
Goes the gun
We're all off now
All different people from different schools.
Some girls in leotards, girls in shorts and T-shirts.
I'm going in the woods, it's starting to rain
I'm halfway through the race now and
I'm really tired and muddy.
I feel like having a hot bath.
I can see the finish line, I'm trying to sprint up
I've finished. I'm so glad.

Hannah Childs (9) Our Lady's RC Combined School

MOVING HOUSE

Moving house is quite scary at first
You miss your house
You miss your garden
But in my case I missed my friends most
for the good times and the bad times
Memories of the old house will never shadow
But every cloud has a silver lining
You meet new friends
Get a new garden
And have more good and bad times

Thomas Hoffman (10) Our Lady's RC Combined School

ME AND MY BROTHER FIGHTING

Me and my brother fighting again,
kicking, shouting, pitching, punching
and screaming again.
My mum and dad come in.
They both shout 'Stop it'.
There's silence for ten minutes.
My mum and dad go out of the room.
They shut the door then we start fighting
again and again

Hayley Brook (10) Our Lady's RC Combined School

HOLIDAY

Yes, I'm going on holiday
With my dad and sister.
I'm going to stay with my grandma and grandad, they really spoil me.
I'm going to bring my bike
I'm going to Ireland where the roads are safe.
And the best thing is I'm missing a day off school!

Joe Murphy (10) Our Lady's RC Combined School

THE DAY WE GO ON HOLIDAY

One more day in England
one more day to Tenerife.
Michelle's annoying me about earplugs
complaining I snore.
My tummy's going up and down,
It's pouring outside I can't wait
to get into the hot sun.

Where are we?
I know we're in Tenerife
But I don't know where in Tenerife
Yes I see the hotel that we're staying in.

We are there we are there
can't wait to get into the pool
Oh it's excellent.

We get to the hotel
and have a look around
My dad brings the cases in
and my mum gets the key.

Caroline Lapperton (10) Our Lady's RC Combined School

THE FIRST TIME

The first time moving to a new country
and a new experience, flying in a plane for 12 hours,
just looking out of the window in the plane looking
at the water.
Then I feel a bump. I shouted 'We're here.
We're here!'
The first thing I noticed was how big the
airport is. I said to myself, 'I think I will like it
here.'

Matthew Parry (9) Our Lady's RC Combined School

WAITING IN A ROOM

Waiting in a room for a music exam.
Your tummy feels funny, your fingers feel numb.
What if I make a mistake. 'Don't worry' says mum.

The person before me, walks out of the door.
I'm thinking, O God help me,
I nearly fall on the floor.

I'm sitting at the piano, he's asking me to play my scales.
I play them quite well. My mum's probably thinking
what if she fails.

The exam's nearly finished. I've just got to do my
sight reading.
I've finished it now. He said I can go,
I'm thinking *wow*!

Emily Harvey (9) Our Lady's RC Combined School

FUNSIZE CHOCOLATE BAR

When you come home from school
and you want something to eat
You ask your mum for a chocolate bar
and you're really really hungry
Your mum gives you one of those funsize chocolate bars,
the ones that are really small.
And you say to your mum, 'But mum I'm really hungry.'
But your mum says, 'Never mind, it's nearly dinner time.'

Katie Geraghty (10) Our Lady's RC Combined School

PIANO EXAM

You practise for about a year the same pieces
and scales and then finally the day comes.
You dread it and you start worrying in the waiting
room, you worry that your fingers will slip or go stiff
and you will play the wrong notes or not listen to
what the examiner tells you to do.
You also worry about the examiner being horrible
or shouting at you and you think you're going
to have to do the exam three times over.
Then suddenly your name is called out so you
go in.
Then the next thing you know you're playing
your pieces.
When you've finished you don't think you've
passed.
A month later you get a certificate to say
you've passed and you are over the moon.

Hannah Schwerzmann (10) Our Lady's RC Combined School

RIVER

The river flows smoothly,
Lighting up stones as it passed its bed.
We can play in the river as happily as can be,
Seizing fishes for our tea.

Nicola Fox (10) Robertswood County Combined School

JOURNEY TO THE SEA

From the gurgling spring I spurt,
Whispering and babbling
Murmuring and tinkling
Swirling and swift,
Toward the cascading fall
Then, overbalancing and landing with a crash
On the rocks below.
Spraying with the breeze
Gushing past the rocks
As fish plunge and dive by me
Tired out now,
Plodding and lazy
Going past trees.
Leisurely and unhurried
Twisting with the meander
Then - ahead of me -
I see miles of water -
The sea!
Sun shining from the horizon
As I flow into the bay
My journey is over.

Joanne Gill (10) Robertswood County Combined School

RIVER COURSE

The new-born stream trickles gently down the mountain,
It is very excited as it leaves Mother Earth for the first time,
Just like a toddler it tumbles over the pebbles,
It meets other little streams and soon makes friends,
It learns to rush on with the main river,
Growing faster and bigger as it gets stronger,
Carrying the stones along,
Eroding the river bed,
It is now quite big and has long since left its mother,
Its sharp ears pick out the distant roar of a waterfall,
It energetically crashes over the sheer cliff,
Wearing away the soft limestone,
It pauses awhile to swish and swirl,
Then hurries on,
It is now getting old and tired,
It slowly meanders across the flatter land,
Tired and weary it gets slower and slower and slower,
Tired and weary it gets closer and closer to its mouth,
Tired and weary it gets wider and wider and wider,
Until eventually,
In its old age,
It is no longer strong enough to carry its cargo,
Weary and tired it joins the vast sea.

Hayley Mitchell (10) Robertswood County Combined School

JOURNEY TO THE SEA

Water runs quickly out of its source,
Starting its long journey to the mouth of the sea.
Crashing down waterfalls,
Bouncing off meanders,
Flowing through rapids,
Then slowing right down and coming to rest.

Thomas Duffy (10) Robertswood County Combined School

THE RIVER BED - MAY IT REST IN PIECES

Here we lie in our watery grave,
While the cool water rushes over our
sleek surface.
Watery we lie in our grave,
while the ice water carries us down the river.
How I do miss the fresh air and sunshine
I used to be so fond of.
And now I only think 'Here lies the river bed
may it rest in pieces.'
And in the end we are all dropped into a
long and wide mouth.
Some of us are swept away into a pit of a
stomach or beyond.
And in the end we are only called a river bed.

Greg Roberts (10) Robertswood County Combined School

FLOWING

When it's young it splashes about,
With a tingling feeling when you bathe in it.
As it gets wider it starts to roar,
And suddenly gushes down into a zooming dive.
The greenish-blue water starts to get stronger,
And the swift, rolling liquid hungrily eats up fishes.
It starts to swirl and wiggle,
As it winds round the sharp bends.

Danny Parton (10) Robertswood County Combined School

THE GREAT WIDE RIVER

From its high source the wide clear
river slowly meanders its way across the
countryside.

It looks clear and majestic, it is pure,
with fishes of all colour swimming in
shoals.

The river then comes to the town,
it becomes black and dirty, and dark

Then the river reaches the sea, it
flows out, dropping everything.

Fram Dinshaw (10) Robertswood County Combined School

RIVER AND THE WATERFALL

The waterfall gushed down into
the sea.
The river rushed into the stream.
The sun beamed down into the
sea.
When you sit by the river it's
cool and sweet and when
it rains you get dreaming pools
of water.

Charlotte Miles (10) Robertswood County Combined School

WATERFALL

The waterfall is cool,
The waterfall sparkles,
It rushes down a big big slope.

It only calms down till dark,
The water drops drip drip drip,
The waterfall is a dreaming thing,
Never stops and does a thing.

Louise Hosier (9) Robertswood County Combined School

RISING WATER

Gates open, let go the impatient water,
trickle down,
tinkly flowing down the hillside.
Sprinkling the grass like a shower,
twists and curves, but very slowly
in a sleeping dream of a pool.
Then the plunge you can hear
the foam rumbling like your tummy.
Gushing down a drop it's clasping
the rocks,
refreshing like a cold drink, but
then it's all ended.

Stephanie Haslam (10) Robertswood County Combined School

THE WATERFALL

Crashing
Bashing
Thundering
down
Like reckless monsters.
Speedy
Swift
Fast
and quick
the waterfall
going
down
down
down.

Tom Beck (10) Robertswood County Combined School

THE WATERFALL

It starts as rapids fast and speedy
It gets reckless and wild
It gets near the plunge
Getting careless now
Crash banging into rocks
           and
           down
           down
           down
           down
           down
       the water went
          splash!

Tom Kirkbride (9) Robertswood County Combined School

THE JOURNEY OF A RIVER

The river went gurgle
The river went turn, turn.
It's the journey of a river
And it twirls on its way.
It goes splish, splash on
the waterfall.
It's trying to get to the
Sea so big and blue.
When it gets there it
is free, after all those years.

Ben Doyle (10) Robertswood County Combined School

HARVEST IS FOR EVERYONE

Fields bright and golden
With crops all gay and bright
Red, red juicy apples in the orchard,
Ooh my tum rumbles in delight.

But people are hungry,
People are sad
Harvest is for everyone
So share your food
Then not only would they be happy
You should be happy too.

Virginia Follen (10) Robertswood County Combined School

RIVER

Flowing free,
Into the sea,
Running along the bed,
Children's toes stepping into the river getting quite a shock!
Gliding past the occupied roads,
In and out the turning corners,
Swiftly passing all the creatures as I go.

Rebecca Galustian (10) Robertswood County Combined School

WATERFALL

The cool spray showers my face with such a refreshing sensation,
    Its clear shallow cleansing swirl mesmerises me.
The effervescence of the dazzling chute is glamour, to my taste.
    Help us Lord to keep this astonishing fall in the land of the living.

Sophia Collins (9) Robertswood County Combined School

THE MOUTH

The mouth gets wider and wider
Till it acquine and unfastens
So the rising water goes through the mouth
Then it gets slower and slower
Then it stops and moves around everywhere.

Olivia De'ath (9) Robertswood County Combined School

HURLING HIGH, SWIRLING LOW

Hurling his waters high
Swirling his waters low
Flowing like a ribbon
Twisting like a ribbon
Rushing, gushing
Waterfalls cascading
And tumbling
The angry river.
The water meandering
Flowing swiftly
Wiggling his way around
The calm peaceful river.

Charlotte Richardson (10) Robertswood County Combined School

HURLING RIVER

Sometimes whirling.
Hurling high.
Sometimes gently rushing by

The rich and sweet powerful river.
Always seeking its way around,
Swiftly passing by.

Flying droplets chilling and fresh.
Cool and shiny.

Samantha Earle (10) Robertswood County Combined School

SWISHY RIVER

Swishing quickly, swishing slowly.
Swishing quickly as fast as I can go,
Azure are my waters,
Young and wanted I am.
Helping boats from town to town.
Curly, whirly I can be,
Swishing slowly, swishing quickly.

Jonathan Slupek (9) Robertswood County Combined School

THE WORLD WAS CRAZY

If the world was crazy,
He-Man would be king,
Lord of all he surveys,
King of everything.

His cape of tin cans,
Bright orange and red,
And of pie dishes royal,
Should be his bed.

Then one day while ruling the land,
Skeletor came and planned,
He-Man would fall today,
Killed without a say.

So that night,
In deepest plight,
He-Man was attacked,
But He-Man saved the day,
And Skeletor was slain.

David Lynch (10) Seer Green Combined School

THE MODERN EXAM

As I waited in my house,
For my Dad,
Pacing up and down around the house.
Mum cursing Dad,
Going to kill him,
Trying to remember
When he last went off in the car.
You see, I'm going to a dance exam.
Miss Steel, my teacher will kill me,
This is my last and only chance to get it right.
I need the car,
We could take the van,
And I'll drive . . .
Phew! Here comes Dad.
He's going to be dead
He's probably forgotten,
Knowing him.
We speed along the motorway,
Going over the limit.
The exam's at 10.00,
It's now 10 to 10.
Help!
Phew, we're here
I've got to get changed,
Wish me luck,
I'm going in
I think I'm going to be sick!

Laura Young (11) Seer Green Combined School

DYE

When my sister dyed her hair,
She found that the colour dye wasn't there.
So she sent me down to the local store,
So I could buy her two packs more.
But instead of getting a colour fair,
She now has got bright green hair.
Thank God I wasn't there,
When in the mirror she did stare!

Kathryn Brodie & Victoria Phillips (11) Seer Green Combined School

FIRE

Sparks, dazzling and dancing, dodging.
Everywhere red, orange, yellow, blue glints
Of *fire*!

Sparkling, beautiful, spectacular.
But, always there is a horror.
A horror of the fire.
The smouldering of rubber and wood.

Sending out a deadly gas, people fainting.
Paramedics carrying them off like the undertaker.

When will the fire be put out?
When can the terror be forgotten?

Anissa Benahmed (10) Seer Green Combined School

LIFE

The pale pink sky looms behind the trees,
As the red sun sets.
The fishermen out at sea,
Have nothing in their nets
The colours of disappointment fill the sky
For all hope is lost.
These fish are free to swim away,
From this cold and bitter frost.
Now families gather round the fire
To bring them warmth and pleasure.
And through every winter we'll survive
Because love is the greatest treasure.

Aleesha Adams (11) Seer Green Combined School

THE RADIATOR GHOST

In my class there is a ghost
and the sound of it is quite gross
it hides in the radiator day and night
and gives everyone a great big fright.

One day I went to look for the teacher
and the ghost said 'Glad to meet ya'
and when I was about to hide
it said 'Why do you look so surprised?'

Rowena Webber (11) Stanton Middle School

AUTUMN NIGHTS

As I staggered along the street
I could feel the bellowing wind
blowing into my face and through
my hair.

As the moon crept out from behind
the clouds I listened to the crackling
of the leaves.

As I looked up at the stars I
could see a faint mist coming
this way for the night.

I crept slowly and softly along
the glistening street as the autumn
wind whispered to the trees.

Vicky Lockwood (11) Stanton Middle School

A WINTER'S MORNING

One cold and beautiful morning,
I saw a lovely landscape of a river from my bedroom
window,
a river flowing through the village town.
Little robins were here and there.
I went outside on the crunchy grass with
diamonds and crystals on the trees.
The bushes were sparkling in the winter's sun.

Kirsten Illsley (9) Stanton Middle School

WINTER'S MORNING

The air was very sharp.
When you breathed there was a
cloud of steam.
The grass and the bushes were
sparkling like diamonds.
It smelt very fresh and cold
on your nose.
When you walked along the
grass it crackled a lot.
When you breathed on the twigs
the frost melted slowly.

Stacy Hodgson (9) Stanton Middle School

WINTER'S MORNING

It was very cold on a winter's morning.
The air was freshly cold.
My fingers were frozen and paralysed.
The grass was sparkling gold.
I was shivering in the snow.
The leaves were in the snow.

Andrew Choy (9) Stanton Middle School

A WINTER MORNING

Frostbite on your fingers.
Apple colour grass and icing sugar
frost!
Glistening sunlight on the frosty
white trees.
Icy clouds of white breath.
Red robins in the trees.
You can see the ice and feel the
breeze.
Fresh smelling air around you.
Black ice and white frost.
Jack has been.
Sharp teeth on the thorn bush
that's up on the heath.

Laura Dennis (10) Stanton Middle School

WINTER MORNING

The trees are shaking just
like us.
While spiky grass is pricking
our freezing hands.
The rough strong wind is
sharp and cold.
Why, the tingly frost is
numbing our toes!
The field is glowing like
jewels and gems.
The slippery ground is
shining in the pretty sunlight.

Stephanie Rounce (10) Stanton Middle School

A WINTER'S MORNING

The trees are shaking just like us.
While spiky grass is pricking our freezing
hands.
The rough strong wind is sharp and cold,
while the tingly is numbing our
toes.
The fields look like a sheet of silver
paper.
The ground is shining in the sunlight.

Alan Clem (9) Stanton Middle School

WINTER MORNING

The grass was covered in sparkling
diamonds.
Ponds were covered with silver glass.
Birds were fluttering in the silver trees.
The frost bit the windows in the early morning.
The crunching of the grass made me shiver.

Tom Evison (10) Stanton Middle School

WINTER'S MORNING

It was a beautiful frost and
everybody was cold.
The grass was silver covered
in snowy ice.
The trees were white except for
the red berries that shone in
the sunlight.

Becky Hall (9) Stanton Middle School

A WINTER MORNING

I watched the glittering of the
trees,
sparkling of the grass,
twinkling of the leaves,
crunching of the twigs,
and the dripping of the ice.

Craig Allen (10) Stanton Middle School

A WINTER'S MORNING

Snow sheets across the fields.
Glistening diamonds upon the trees.
The strong sun making marshy lands.
Cracking diamonds upon the grass.
Children skating on frozen lakes.
Smell of fresh dew upon the plants.
The cold damp air makes you shiver.
Sparkling sunlight upon a badger's set
shining as the sun rises.
I hope Jack Frost will come again.

Teri Slater (10) Stanton Middle School

A WINTER'S MORNING

I watch the glittering of the
trees,
sparkling of the grass,
twinkling of the leaves,
crunching of the twigs and
the dripping of the ice.

Dean Scott (10) Stanton Middle School

WINTER MORNING

On a cold winter morning
I stood on the grass,
It was crunchy and cracking
The trees were like bare skeletons
The field was glistening like diamonds.

Carl Winstanley (10) Stanton Middle School

A WINTER MORNING

It was cold and frosty and
the grass was as sharp as a blade.
I looked at a tree which was bare.
I blew off the frost.
When I spoke out came steam.
I touched the floor which
sparkled galore and which was
as cold as the North Pole.
I looked at the field which was
like a silver sea.

Ian Ritchie (10) Stanton Middle School

WINTER MORNING

The trees that glitter in the sunlight
and the breezy cold wind that makes
you shiver.
The lake shines when morning breaks and
the crackling cold beneath your feet.
Grass on the ground looking like icing on
a cake.
When you breathe it looks like smoke
from a fire.
The trees in the field look like hills of snow
and the bushes that freeze your fingers
when you touch them on a winter's morning.

Hayley Dixon (9) Stanton Middle School

WINTER MORNING

It was cold on a winter's morning.
Frosty and cold lovely plain
White silver windows.
You can feel the fog in
your hands travelling in the air.
Cold and wet grass lovely
and frozen snow to ski on.

Jason Barker (9) Stanton Middle School

WINTER MORNING

On a winter morning it was cold and
frosty in the air.
The ice was like sharp claws digging
down in the ground.
Slowly it broke as it melted.

Brooke Fry (10) Stanton Middle School

A WINTER'S MORNING

The white sparkling landscape of the
fields looks like it is covered with a
giant white blanket.
The sunlight forms sparkles of light on
the ice and frost.
Each breath I take becomes a white cloud
floating in the air then just disappears.
The grass feels crispy and crunches when I
tread.
The prickles on the bush look like sparkling
glass teeth.

Ashley Sharp (10) Stanton Middle School

WINTER'S MORNING

Ice gleaming in the sunlight.
A fresh icy smell everywhere.
Robins perched high in a tree.
Water frozen in the stream.
Ice shimmering in the trees.
Teeth chattering everywhere.

Ben Enser (9) Stanton Middle School

A WINTER MORNING

The grass was frosted and crunchy.
The trees glistened with icicles and diamonds.
My breath was like frosted clouds.
The birds were shivering like cold snowmen.
The trees sparkled like white diamonds.
My hands felt like shivery snow balls.
The frost lay over the winter landscape.

Michael Fanning (9) Stanton Middle School

WINTER MORNING

The sun was shining through the trees.
The grass was glinting like lovely diamonds on the
ground.
The birds were collecting berries from the trees so high.
The grass smelled like fresh grass.
When you walk through the frost it sounds like a
creaking noise.
When you breath it floats into the air like a puff
of smoke.
When you touch the plants it feels icy.

Lyndsey Berrie (10) Stanton Middle School

A WINTER MORNING

I walk outside and my teeth start to chatter.
The grass glistens like white sheets just been
washed.
I breathe and a puffing cloud floats out of my
mouth,
The sun shines and the purple sky is bright,
The frost covers the landscape.

Joanne Green (10) Stanton Middle School

A WINTER MORNING

The sparkling grass shining like a
bunch of diamonds and crystals.
The frosty air filled with puffing clouds.
The melting ice that drips from the
trees when the sun shines brightly.
The little icicles that drip from the
bare trees.
The grass crunches as you walk
across it shivering.

Laura Hammond (10) Stanton Middle School

A WINTER MORNING

It looks like a great big snow
storm has been overnight when I was
asleep.
The grass crackling when I walk on top
of it.
It sounds like paper getting ripped.
I look above, I see the robin flying
and feeding in the trees.
I touch the grass and it feels like
ten ice cubes in my hand.
I look across the fields and I see
the pond filled with ice.
When I walk the ice goes into my
shoes and it feels like an ice cream
is in it.
I look down at the grass and it looks
like a lot of crystals.

Matthew Darton (9) Stanton Middle School

A WINTER MORNING

I woke with the lovely
sunlight shining in.
A robin was singing beautifully
on the side of the wall.
The pavement was full of glitter
and frost.
The pond had frozen over.
My feet were frozen.
The leaves on the trees were
frozen.

Wayne Entwistle (10) Stanton Middle School

WINTER MORNING

The robins perch themselves on top of the
sugar coated trees.

Half of the sunlight and snow covers the
hungry vole and fox.

The bold fox with his crisp coated frosty
nose scans for water snake or goose.

A white sheet of snow covers the land.

Lightning or thunder cannot scratch
for the frost biting snow steals it in
flight.

The full sun comes up for the day.

The fox nor vole dare move today.

Lewis Gardner (10) Stanton Middle School

THE SWAN

Gliding swiftly on the lake,
her white tail swaying to and fro.
Rippling water after her and
down the lake she goes.

Water as clear as crystal
hanging trees all around
suddenly she looks around
to see if her cygnet's are there.

Ellie Wilson (9) Turnfurlong Middle School

THE DOLPHINS SWIMMING IN THE SEA

While on a ramble we wandered slow,
by hills and meadow we did go,
we came across a sunlit bay.
We watched a while, then went close to see
Dolphins swim and glide through clear blue sea
and tide. They came close to light washed
sand. I'm sure simply to allow us to
touch them with our hands.
To our class at least, they were
Gay and sparkling band.

Nicola Cannings (11) Tylers Green Middle School

HEDGEHOGS

You may think hedgehogs
are cuddly and cute.
But the problem is
their spiky suit.

Naomi Telfer (11) Tylers Green Middle School

THE TEACHER

The teacher has a grumpy look
with a solid face
and a bristle eye,
which turns towards my desk.
I gulp!
Then she said to me,
'Stop talking girl and sit down in
your seat.'
'But I have to borrow a pen.'
Now the teacher's steaming red and
what do I do?
I look at Miss Maple who just
walked in the door.
The place goes silent
I bend to sit but miss the chair
and hurt my bum
I want my mum I scream.
She says 'Don't be silly girl'
I grab for the table
and pull myself up.
I reach for the pen.
I've got it!
'Now I'm alright Miss.'

Joanna Thompson (10) Tylers Green Middle School

A RIVER

The water flowing in a river is a lovely thing
to behold.
As it swishes, gurgles and trickles,
All the way down to the sea,
The water seems ageless,
Unlike my Dad and me.

David Witherden (11) Tylers Green Middle School

THE DARK

All alone in my bed
Creepy shapes above my head
The wind is howling through the window
It's dark and I'm afraid.

An owl hoots as he hunts in the night
A dog barks and it gives me a fright
Branches tapping at the window
It's dark and I'm afraid.

The floorboards creak as does the door
I can't take this any more
There's a spider in the corner
It's dark and I'm afraid.

Philippa Taylor (11) Tylers Green Middle School

THE RANKING OF GUNS

A boy called Fred came up to me and said,
'Hey little guy, I'll squirt you with my water pistol and leave you out to dry'
Then my big brother Ted came out and said
'Yer wanna bet, Fred the sick animal needs a vet'
'Nah a potato gun will do, liquid versus solid
I can certainly beat you'
Then the big brother of Fred came out and said
'My BB gun can beat your potato gun, yes it's true.
Get running mate 'cos I would if I was you'
Then my Uncle Ned came out and said
'Got a whole round of bullets in my revolver
£20 was the price they sold it for'
The grandad of Fred came out and said
'Run run from my machine gun'
But it is all fun, fun, fun.

My dad got cross, he came out and said
'How'd ya like my grenade launcher?'
'Wait, don't run, the fun's just begun'
Out comes the dad of Fred, his head poked out of a cockpit. He said
'How do you like my tank? Hey, how do you like my tank?'
Then a copper came round the corner. He said
'Have you got a licence for that mate?'
'I did but it's out of date.'
'For this little trick, you're getting 7 years at the nick.'

Peter Thorne (11) Tylers Green Middle School

THE PLANT

I had a plant which was quite small,
then suddenly it grew up the wall.
It went through the house next door,
through their kitchen door.

Soon it conquered the whole street
which made the ladies jump to their feet.

People came from miles around
to see what landed on the ground.

It was the most peculiar plant you see,
with fruit and vegetables on the same tree.

Along came a man from the BBC
he came along to interview me.

He asked me what I'd given it to grow
I said I didn't know!

I then saw the man next door
who was lying on the floor
with shock of the plant I think
but I didn't want to think.

I then woke up with such a fright
the plant was going to eat me
but it was in the middle of the night.

The plant was in my dream you see
there was no man from the BBC.

Hannah Jeffries (11) Tylers Green Middle School

A PUZZLE POEM

I sit in the corner for days and days
And nobody notices my little ways.

Then suddenly I spring to life,
Whizzing around as if I'm in flight.

I get all excited, and then look around
And see all the things that are left on the ground.

I suddenly realise, I feel a bit ill,
There's a pain in my tummy, I must be filled.

I am turned upside down, off come my prickles,
Someone's taking a look - ooh that tickles!

The trouble is obvious, I am ready to bust
It just has to be something to do with the dust.

At last someone's noticed, they're changing my bag
Oh hang on a minute! They're having a fag.

I have been like this for hours, and now I'm repaired,
I just had that feeling, I knew someone cared.

I am ready to go, the action has started,
Now I'm turned off, but it was good whilst it lasted.

I am rolled away, back to the gloom,
Back to the corner of my little room.

Have you guessed what I am, I am quite a good mover,
Yes, you've guessed it, I am a *Hoover*!

Charlotte V Ellis (10) Tylers Green Middle School

WAR

Soldiers marching close to death.
Guns shooting, bombs blasting
Death approaches.
Bullets fired, planes flying.
Tanks crushing, supplies supplying.
Boots stamping, swords clashing
Death is close.
Peace is arriving, peace is here.
Buildings rebuilt, streets repaired
Families reunited
Everyone loses,
Nobody wins.

Stephen Eakins (11) Tylers Green Middle School

INFORMATION

We hope you have enjoyed reading this book - and that you will continue to enjoy it in the coming years.

If you like reading and writing poetry drop us a line, or give us a call, and we'll send you a free information pack.

Write to

        Poetry Now (Young Writers) Information
        1-2 Wainman Road
        Woodston
        Peterborough
        PE2 7BU